W9-CKL-691

A Hole Is To Dig

A FIRST BOOK OF FIRST DEFINITIONS

by

Ruth Krauss

Pictures by

Maurice Sendak

A Harper Trophy Book
HARPER & ROW, PUBLISHERS

Thanks to a number of children and teachers in the
Harriet Johnson Nursery School; and special thanks
to children in the Rowayton School Kindergarten,
and their teacher, Harriet S. Sherman.

Mashed potatoes are to
give everybody enough

A face is so you can make faces

A face is something to have
on the front of your head

Dogs are to kiss people

Hands are to hold

A hand is to
hold up when
you want your tur

A hole is to dig

The ground is
to make a garden

Grass is to cut

Grass is to have on
the ground with dirt under it
and clover in it

Maybe you
could hide things
in a hole

A party is to say how-do-you-d
and shake hands

A party is to make
little children happy

Arms are to hug with

Toes are to wiggle

Ears are to wiggle

Mud is to jump in and slide in and
yell doodleedoodleedoo

Anh-h-h-

Doodleedoodleedoo-oo!

A castle is to build
in the sand

A hole is to sit in

A dream is to look at the night
and see things

Snow is to roll in

Buttons are to
keep people warm

The world is so
you have something
to stand on

The sun is to tell you when
it's every day

When you make your bed
you get a star

Grr-r-r

Little stones are for little children
to gather up and put in little piles

Oo! A rock
is when you trip on it
you should have watched where
you were going

Children are to

A brother is to help you

A principal
is to take out
splinters

A mountain is to go
to the top

A mountain is
to go to the bottom

A lap is so you
don't get crumbs
on the floor

A mustache is to
wear on Halloween

A hat is to wear on a train

Toes are to dance on

Eyebrows are to
go over your eyes

A sea shell is to hear the sea

A wave is to wave bye-bye

Big shells are to put
little shells in

A hole is to plant a flower

A watch is to hear it tick

Dishes are to do

Cats are so you can have kittens

Mice are to
eat your cheese

Noses are to rub

A nose is to blow

A match is to blow

A whistle is to make people jump

Rugs are so you don't get splinters in you

Boodlyboodly

A floor is so you
don't fall in the hole
your house is in

Hunh! Rugs are so
dogs have napkins

A hole is
for a mouse
to live in

A door is to open

A door is to shut

A hole is
to look through

Steps are to sit on

A hole is
when you step in it
you go down

Hands are to make things

Hands are to eat with

A tablespoon is to eat a table with

A package is to look inside

The sun is so it can be a great day

A book
is to look at